Renaissance Patterns for Lace, Embroidery and Needlepoint

Renaissance Patterns for Lace, Embroidery and Needlepoint

AN UNABRIDGED FACSIMILE OF THE 'SINGULIERS
ET NOUVEAUX POURTRAICTS' OF 1587

by Federico Vinciolo

DOVER PUBLICATIONS, INC., NEW YORK

Published in Canada by General Publishing Company, Ltd., 30 Lesmill Road, Don Mills, Toronto, Ontario.
Published in the United Kingdom by Constable and Company, Ltd., 10 Orange Street, London WC 2.

This Dover edition, first published in 1971, is an unabridged republication of a 1909 facsimile edition of Federico Vinciolo's *Les singuliers et nouveaux pourtraicts . . . pour toutes sortes d'ouvrages de Lingerie,* a work originally published in Paris by Jean Leclerc in 1587. The facsimile is based on a 1606 printing of the third edition (the first printing of this edition was also in 1587). The facsimile was originally published in 1909, with the title *I singolari e nuovi disegni per lavori di biancheria,* by the Istituto Italiano d'Arti Grafiche in Bergamo in their series *Libri Antichi di Modelli* (Old Pattern Books), subseries *Merletti e Ricami* (Lace and Embroidery).

The 1909 editor's preface (originally in Italian) and the full French text of the original work have been translated specially for the present edition by Stanley Appelbaum.

DOVER *Pictorial Archive* SERIES

International Standard Book Number: 0-486-22438-4
Library of Congress Catalog Card Number: 79-121586

Manufactured in the United States of America
Dover Publications, Inc.
180 Varick Street
New York, N.Y. 10014

Editor's Preface

To judge by the number of times this little book by Vinciolo was reprinted between 1587 and 1658,* the cultured and critical ladies of the time presumably considered it the best of its type.

We have knowledge of some seventeen editions; but there is reason to believe that there were more, since it is inconceivable that some fragment or some recollection of every edition has come down to us, considering the manner in which ladies would use, or rather consume, such pattern books, ripping out the leaves and distributing them to their needlewomen, just as one does today with the patterns found in fashion periodicals.

The first edition published in France bears the date 1587. But the dedicatory epistle of the printer Leclerc, in which he mentions patterns he had found earlier in Italy, leads us to assume the existence of a previous edition printed in Italy. In fact, after saying: "the man who can bring back something new from foreign countries considers himself happy to present it to some great personage," he adds that, "having brought back from Italy some rare and unusual patterns," he presents them to Her Majesty the Queen of France.

This quite explicit statement by the publisher perhaps escaped the notice of d'Adda and Alvin, who, instead of entertaining the notion of an earlier Italian edition, firmly considered the 1589 and 1658 Turin editions (sixty-nine years apart) as pirated versions, done at Lyons, of the Parisian edition.

Alvin is led to this conclusion by the fact that this book by Vinciolo, unlike the others of its type, has its title, dedications and captions written in French, even in the Turin reprints made by Eleazar Thomyssi. But this should not surprise any one who knows how widely used French was, and

---

* The old editions of *Singuliers et nouveaux pourtraicts* known today are as follows: 1587, Paris, Jean Leclerc (three editions); 1588, Paris, Jean Leclerc; 1589, Turin, Eleazar Thomyssi; 1589, Paris; 1595, Paris, Jean Leclerc; 1596, Paris, Jean Leclerc; 1597, Liège, Jean de Glen; 1599, Basel, Louis Roy; 1601, Paris, Jean Leclerc; 1603, Paris, Jean Leclerc; 1603, Lyons, Léonard Odet; 1612, Paris, Jean Leclerc; 1613, Paris, Jean Leclerc; 1623, Paris, Veuve [Widow] Leclerc; 1658, Turin, Eleazar Thomyssi.

still is, in Turin (from proximity and for political reasons) among the higher classes, for whom these books were intended. Moreover, in the present case, the author speaks of himself on the title page as "Seigneur Federic [sic] de Vinciolo Venitien," and the designs are clearly Italian in style.

Vinciolo was probably summoned or brought to Paris by that same Catherine de Médicis who was the first to teach France the art of fine Italian lacemaking, and who, at her death, left behind in her chests nearly a thousand *carrés de réseuil* [squares of net embroidery] similar to those in the second part of this book. In fact, Catherine granted Federico Vinciolo the exclusive right to manufacture those enormous starched ruffs (*fraises*) which the Italian queen had made fashionable in Paris.

At any rate there is no doubt that *Les singuliers et nouveaux pourtraicts* was received very favorably from its first appearance, since in 1587 alone it ran to three editions; in 1589 it was reprinted simultaneously in Turin and in Paris; and almost a century later, even after the publication of Cesare Vecellio's *Corona* and the books by Franco, Isabella Catanea Parasole, Danieli and others, it was still being reprinted.

Nor was the supreme sanction denied to the success of the book: it was plagiarized.

One Jean Baptiste de Glen, doctor of theology, published at Liège in 1597 a treatise entitled *Du debvoir des filles* (On the Duty of Girls). His brother Jean de Glen, printer and wood engraver, followed up the moral and hygienic precepts with . . . *Les singuliers et nouveaux pourtraicts*, in which all, or nearly all, of Vinciolo's book, from the title on down, is reproduced, including the sonnet, which is there dedicated not "aux dames et damoiselles" in general, but to "Loyse Perez espouse a [wife of] M. Charles de Billehé."

Vinciolo's name is omitted, but despite this the colophon at the end of the pirated volume boldly proclaims the motto "Cuique sua proemia" [To each his rewards].

Vinciolo's little book is the first among those known to us which contains nothing but lace designs, whereas the earlier books alternate these with designs for all kinds of needlework; it is also the first book to offer patterns for *reticella* ("Greek" lace) and *punto in aria* (guipure) without a geometric outline. Perhaps there is a lacuna between the *point coupé* designs of Giovanni Ostans (1567) and those of Vinciolo (1587), because the style and the very technique of the work seem too radically changed.

Some designer between Ostans and Vinciolo, who has left no trace, probably pointed the way to be followed later by Vecellio, Parasole, Danieli and the others, who appear today as imitators of our Vinciolo. Not always discreet imitators, for these old designers had more imagination and good taste than conscience, and did not scruple to pick some flower from some one else's garden in order to enrich their own *Corone* (Wreathes), or *Preziose gemme* (Precious Gems) or *Ghirlande* (Garlands).*

In the second part the designs are for works in square netting (lacis) or *buratto* (embroidery on cloth). The designs for lacis are clearly divided into regular little squares, and were copied by counting the meshes; on the other hand, the patterns for *buratto* (see the plates with Sol, Luna, Mars, Mercury, Jupiter, Venus, Saturn, etc.), with their freer forms, were meant to be transferred to the cloth and worked in darning stitch into the thin and transparent weave of colored silk or white thread: a cloth that is called, precisely, *buratto*.

ELISA RICCI

We owe the pleasure of initiating our series of Old Pattern Books with this important and rare work to Mr. van Overloop, Director of the Royal Museum of Decorative and Industrial Arts, Brussels, who kindly allowed us to reproduce the valuable copy he aquired a few years ago for the museum library.

* The plate with the pelican reappears almost unchanged in Vecellio, and many other motifs from Vinciolo recur in later works.

Bibliography

LEOPOLDO CICOGNARA: *Catalogo di libri d'arte e d'antichi pizzi*. Pisa, 1821.

PIETRO ZANI: *Enciclopedia metodica delle Belle Arti*, part 1, vol. XIX, p. 194. Parma, 1824.

DE REIFFENBERG (DE RG.): *Impression liégeoise inconnue en partie ou du moins mal connue* in *Bulletin du bibliophile belge*. Brussels, 1845.

GIROLAMO D'ADDA: *Essai sur les anciens modèles de lingerie*, in *Gazette des Beaux Arts*, vol. XVII, pp. 425 and 430. Paris, 1863.

L. ALVIN: *Les anciens patrons de Broderies, de Dentelle et de Guipure* in *Echo du Parlement*. Brussels, 28 Dec. 1862 and 5 Jan. 1863.

Translations

page 1

The Unusual and New Designs, by Signor Federico [de] Vinciolo, Venetian, for all sorts of needlework. / Dedicated to the Dowager Queen of France. / To which have again and for the third time been added—over and above the primary network, *point coupé* [cutwork in geometric designs] and lacis [darned netting]—several beautiful and different designs for network with counted stitches, giving the number of meshes, something never before seen or invented. / Paris, for Jean Leclerc, rue St.-Jean de Latran, at the sign of the Royal Salamander. / With the King's license. 1606.

page 2

LATIN INSCRIPTION ON KING'S PORTRAIT

Henri III, by the Grace of God, King of France and Poland

TRANSLATION OF VERSES

Painter, if you would vie with Nature's workmanship
In limning of this king whose honors reach the skies,
Paint Pallas on his head, Mercury on his lip,
Mars on his countenance, and Love within his eyes.

page 3

PREFACE TO THE READER, BY SIGNOR FEDERICO [DE] VINCIOLO

I believe that you are not unaware, kind reader, what a great and pains-taking task I earlier undertook to depict and publish the large number of excellent needlework patterns contained in the present book, which, as was only just, were dedicated to Her Majesty the Queen. And yet, although I spent a long time in the invention of this work, and in the investigation and careful rendering of all the stitches of each design, nevertheless, being duly apprised of the utility and profit I have by so doing given to many who by this means have derived uncommon pleasure in imitating these designs, it seemed to me that I would still have accomplished nothing, if I did not in addition announce to you a new group of designs which I promised you when this book was first printed. Therefore, in order not to break my promise to you, and in order to comply with the grievances of some ladies who have complained that I had attempted only idly to furnish them with network patterns as beautiful as they desired, I have decided to invent and set before your eyes for the third time several new and different network designs with counted stitches, which I have sewn and attached at the end of my earlier illustrations, as you will see when you give them your particular attention; beneath these new designs, to afford you greater ease of understanding and to spare you trouble, I have noted the number and quantities of meshes that each design may have and contain. Moreover, I assure you that I think I have forgotten nothing, as far as it lay in my power, to make their presentation beautiful and pleasant to your eyes; requesting you, in case there should perhaps be some not as beautiful as you would wish, not on that account to condemn my work or the good will I bear toward the French nation, which I pray God may succor at all times.

page 4

LATIN INSCRIPTION ON QUEEN'S PORTRAIT

Louise of Lorraine, Queen of France

Godfathered by three gods was Henry Third the King:
Jupiter, Phoebus, Mars. Three goddesses were fain
To bless Louise's birth, that fair pearl of Lorraine:
Pallas, Venus, the Grace who blooms in endless spring.

page 5

TO THE QUEEN

Madame, the man who can bring back something new from foreign countries considers himself happy to present it to some great personage, knowing that by so doing he affords him more pleasure than if he gave him something common, even if it were of great price and value. Thus, having brought back from Italy some rare and unusual patterns and designs for needlework, and having invented some others, as far as my small knowledge permitted, I thought, inasmuch as those matters pertain principally to the ladies, that perchance I would not do ill to put myself forward and take the liberty of presenting them to Your Majesty, not only so that you might derive some pleasure therefrom, but also because I would like every one to know that if these patterns and designs bring some profit and utility to France (as I am assured they will, seeing that some others less perfect and more crudely sketched have been useful and profitable before now), France will be chiefly indebted to you for this, because I have prepared them for your inspection and in order to satisfy your eyes, which are so gracious and noble that they will gladly deign to look upon the work and the workman, who desires nothing more than to produce something which which will give them pleasure. In the hope that you will accept these inventions, to which I expect to add for you shortly, with the help of God, several other different patterns and designs, I pray God, Madame, to give you a long and happy life and the fulfillment of your noble desires.

Your most humble and obedient servant and subject,
Leclerc.

TO THE LADIES AND YOUNG MISSES

Sonnet

One man will strive to win the heart of some liege lord
In order to possess a sum of riches great;
Another in high rank himself would situate;
Another in the wars will seek for his reward.

But I, who only seek to keep from being bored,
Am satisfied to live in this my lowly state,
And by my labors grave strive only to create
A gift for womankind, contentment to afford.

Then, ladies, please accept (I pray you will so do)
These patterns and designs I dedicate to you,
To while away your time and occupy your mind.

In this new enterprise there's much that you can learn,
And finally this craft you'll master in your turn.
The work agreeable, the profit great you'll find.

> To die unremittingly for virtue
> is not to die.

Renaissance Patterns for Lace, Embroidery and Needlepoint

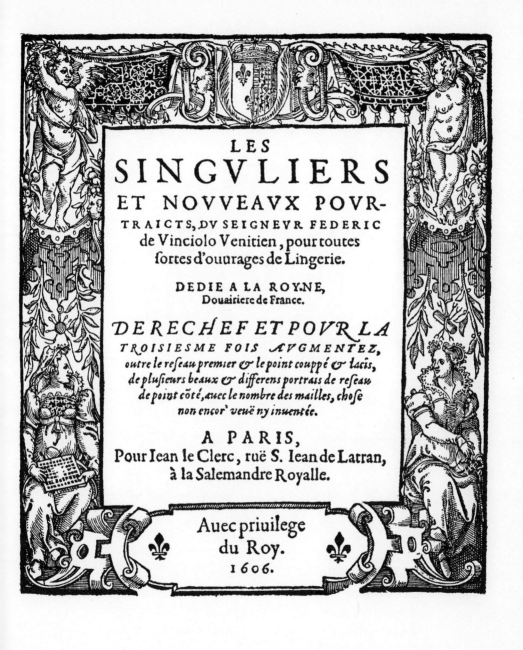

LES
SINGVLIERS
ET NOVVEAVX POVR-
TRAICTS, DV SEIGNEVR FEDERIC
de Vinciolo Venitien, pour toutes
sortes d'ouurages de Lingerie.

DEDIE A LA ROY·NE,
Douairiere de France.

DE RECHEF ET POVR LA
TROISIESME FOIS AVGMENTEZ,
outre le reseau premier & le point couppé & lacis,
de plusieurs beaux & differens portraits de reseau
de point côté, auec le nombre des mailles, chose
non encor' veuë ny inuentée.

A PARIS,
Pour Iean le Clerc, ruë S. Iean de Latran,
à la Salemandre Royalle.

Auec priuilege
du Roy.
1606.

Peintre a fin que ton art imite la Nature,
Au tableau de ce Roy dont l'honneur touche aux Cieux,
Pein sur son chef Pallas, sur ses léures Mercure,
Mars deſſus son viſage, & l'amour dans ses yeux.

ADVERTISEMENT A
LECTEVR PAR LE SEIGNEVR
Federic de Vinciolo.

E croy que tu n'ignores point (amy Lecteur) quel grand & penible labeur i'ay peu prendre à cy deuant dépaindre & mettre en lumiere, grande quantite d'excellens patrons d'ouurages contenus en ce present liure, lesquels pour équitablemeut approprier la chose, ont esté dediez à la Majesté de la Royne: Et toutesfois bien que i'ay cōsommé vne longue espace de temps à l'inuention de cet œuure, & à recercher & subtiliser soigneusement tous les poins de chacun portrait, si est-ce qu'estant deuëment certioré de l'vtilité & profit que i'ay apporté en ce faisant à plusieurs, qui par mesme moyē ont pris singulier plaisir à imiter lesdits portraits: Il m'a semblé qu'encores ie n'auoy rien fait, si d'abondant ie ne te faisois part d'vne autre nouuelle bande d'ouurages laquelle ie t'auoy promise des la premiere impression de ce liure. A ceste cause, pour ne te manquer de promesse, & subuenir aux doléaces de quelques Dames, qui se sont plaintes que ie m'estoy amusé à leur depaindre du reseau assez beau à leur fantasie, i'ay bien voulu pour la troisiesme fois inuenter & mettre deuant tes yeux, plusieurs nouueaux & differens portrais de reseau de point côté, que i'ay cousus & attachez à la fin de mes premieres figures comme tu pourras voir en les particularisant, au dessous desquels pour plus grande & facile intelligences, & te releuer de peine, i'ay mis le nōbre & la quantité des mailles que chacun portrait peut auoir & contenir. Au demeurát ie t'asseure que ie ne pense y auoir rien oublié de mon pouuoir, pour te les rendre & representer beaux & agréables à l'œil. Te priant que s'il s'en trouue quelqu'vn, qui ne soit peut-estre si beau que tu le desires, ne côdamner pour cela mon œuure, ni la bonne volonté que ie porte à la nation Frāçoise, à laquelle ie prie Dieu estre en tout temps secourable.

Trois Dieux furent parreins du troisiefme Henry,
Iupiter, Mars, Phebus; cette perle Lorraine,
Vne triple Deèffe eut pour triple marreine,
Palas, Venus, la grace au chef toufiours fleury.

A LA ROYNE.

ADAME, celuy qui peut recouurer quelque chose nouuelle des pays estranges, s'estime bien heureux d'en faire vn
present à quelque grand personnage, sçachant qu'en cela
il le gratifie d'auantage que s'il luy donnoit quelque chose
commune, encor qu'elle fust de grand pris & valeur: Ainsi ayant re-
couuré de l'Italie quelques rares & singuliers patrons & ouurages de
l'ingerie, & en ayant inuenté quelques vns, selon mon petit sçauoir,
i'ay pensé, puis que ces choses la appartiennent principalement aux
Dames, que ie ne ferois parauanture mal de m'aduancer & m'enhar-
dir les presenter à vostre Majesté, tant à fin qu'elle y prenne quelque
contentement, que pour le desir que i'ay que chacun connoise que
si ces patrons & pourtraicts ameinent quelque profit & vtilité à la
France, (comme l'on m'asseure qu'ils feront, veu que quelques vns
moins parfaicts, & plus rudement ébauchez ont seruy & profité cy
deuant:) elle vous en doit principalement estre tenue, pource que ie
les ay faicts pour vostre regard, & à fin d'en contenter vostre œil, tant
gracieux & débonnaire, que volontiers il verra l'œuure & l'ouurier,
qui ne desire rien plus que de faire chose qui luy soit agréable; & sous
l'espérance que vous prendrez en gré ces inuentions, que ie m'attens
vous augmenter en brief, Dieu aydent, de plusieurs autres différens
patrons & pourtraits; ie prie Dieu,
Madame vous donner heureuse & longue vie, & l'accomplissement
de vos bons desirs

Vostre tres-humble & tres-obeissant seruiteur
& subiect,   le Clerc.

AVX DAMES

ET DAMOISELLES

SONNET.

 'Vn s'efforce à gaigner le cœur des grands Seigneurs
Pour poſſeder en fin vne exquiſe richeſſe,
L'autre aſpire aux eſtats, pour monter en alteſſe,
Et l'autre, par la guerre allechee les honneurs.

Quand à moy, ſeulemēt pour chaſſer mes lāgueurs,
Ie me ſen ſatisfaict de viure en petiteſſe,
Et de faire ſi bien, qu'aux Dames ie delaiſſe,
Vn grand contentement en mes graues labeurs.

Prenez doncques en gré (mes Dames) ie vous prie
Ces pourtrais ouuragez leſquels ie vous dedie,
Pour tromper vos ennuis, & l'eſprit employer.

En ceſte nouueauté, pourrez beaucoup apprendre,
Et maiſtreſſes en fin en ceſt œuure vous rendre,
Le trauail eſt plaiſant: Si grand eſt le loyer.

Morir aſſidouamente per
virtu, non morirè.

7

Ouurages de point couppe.

Needlework in *point coupé*.

[The 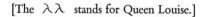 stands for Queen Louise.]

Ouurages de point couppe.

[The escutcheon on the left is that of France,
the H in the other stands for Henri III.]

Ouurages de point couppe.

Ouurages de point couppe.

Ouurages de point couppe.

Ouurages de point couppe.

Ouurages de point couppe.

Ouurages de point couppe.

Ouurages de point couppe.

Ouurages de point couppe.

Ouurages de point couppe.

Ouurages de point couppe.

Ouurages de point couppe.

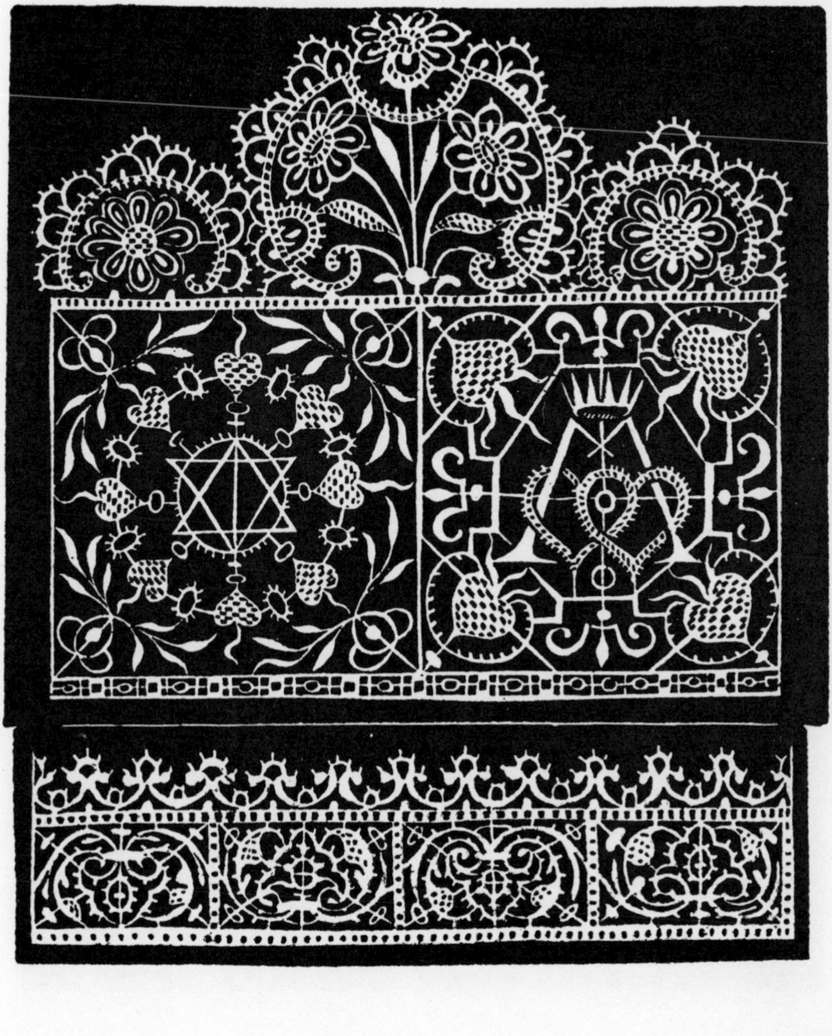

Ouurages de point couppe.

Ouurages de point couppe.

Ouurages de point couppe.

Ouurages de point couppe.

Ouurages de point couppe.

Ouurages de point couppe.

33

35

36

Ouurages de point couppe.

Ouurages de point couppe.

Ouurages de point couppe.

Ouurages de point couppe.

Ouurages de point couppe.

44

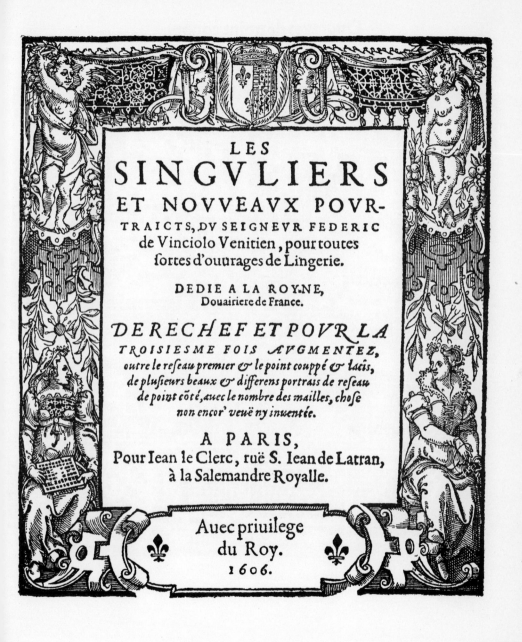

LES
SINGVLIERS
ET NOVVEAVX POVR-
TRAICTS, DV SEIGNEVR FEDERIC
de Vinciolo Venitien, pour toutes
sortes d'ouurages de Lingerie.

DEDIE A LA ROY-NE,
Douairiere de France.

DE RECHEF ET POVR LA
TROISIESME FOIS AVGMENTEZ,
outre le reseau premier & le point couppé & lacis,
de plusieurs beaux & differens portraits de reseau
de point côté, auec le nombre des mailles, chose
non encor' veuë ny inuentée.

A PARIS,
Pour Iean le Clerc, ruë S. Iean de Latran,
à la Salemandre Royalle.

Auec priuilege
du Roy.
1606.

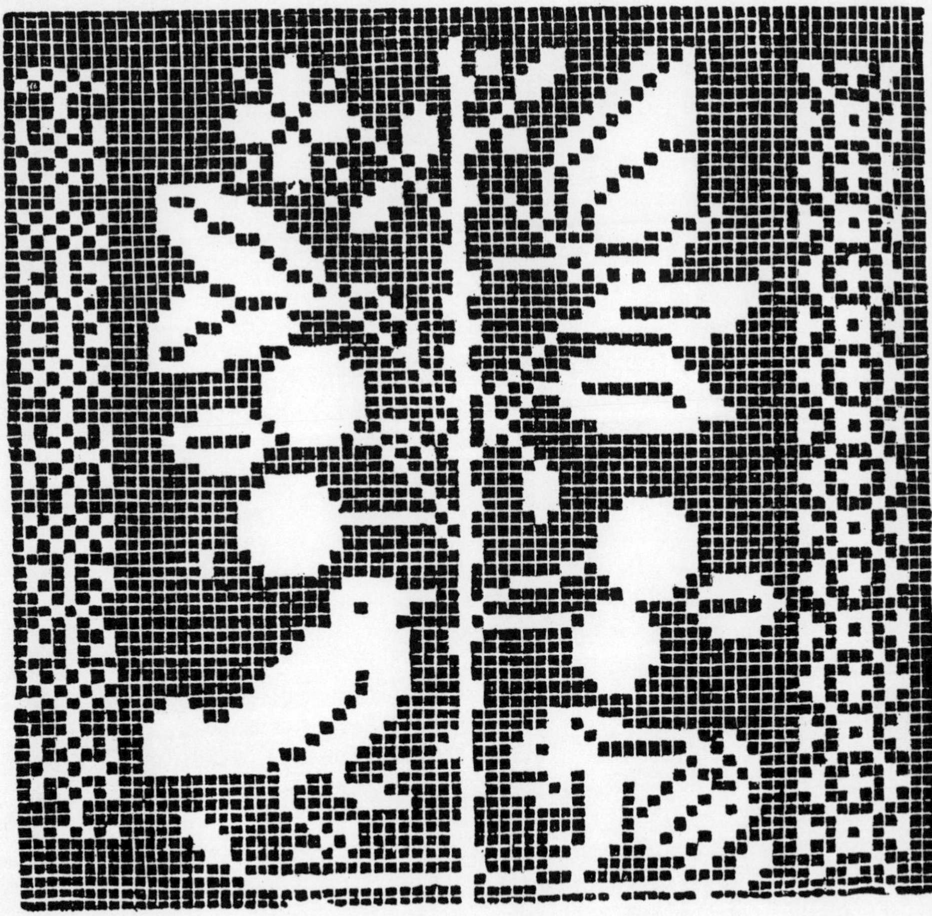

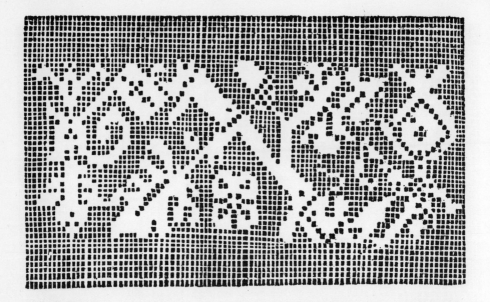

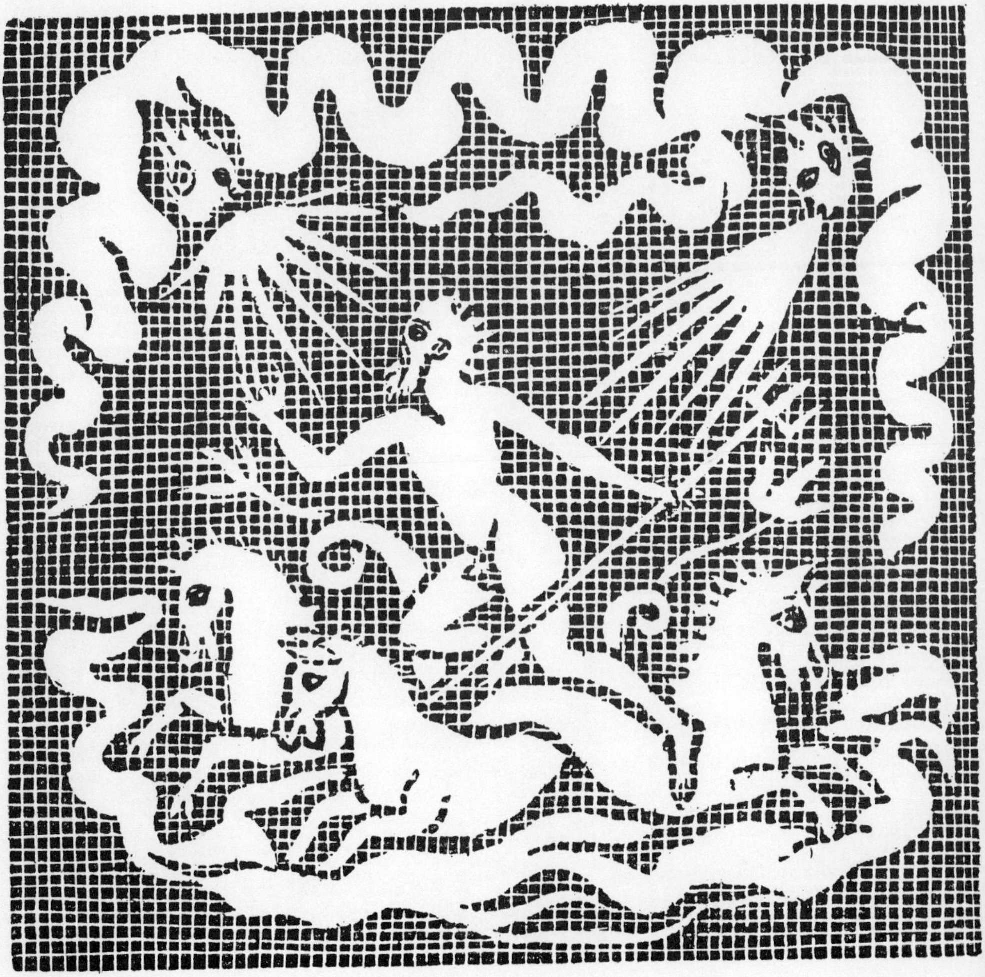

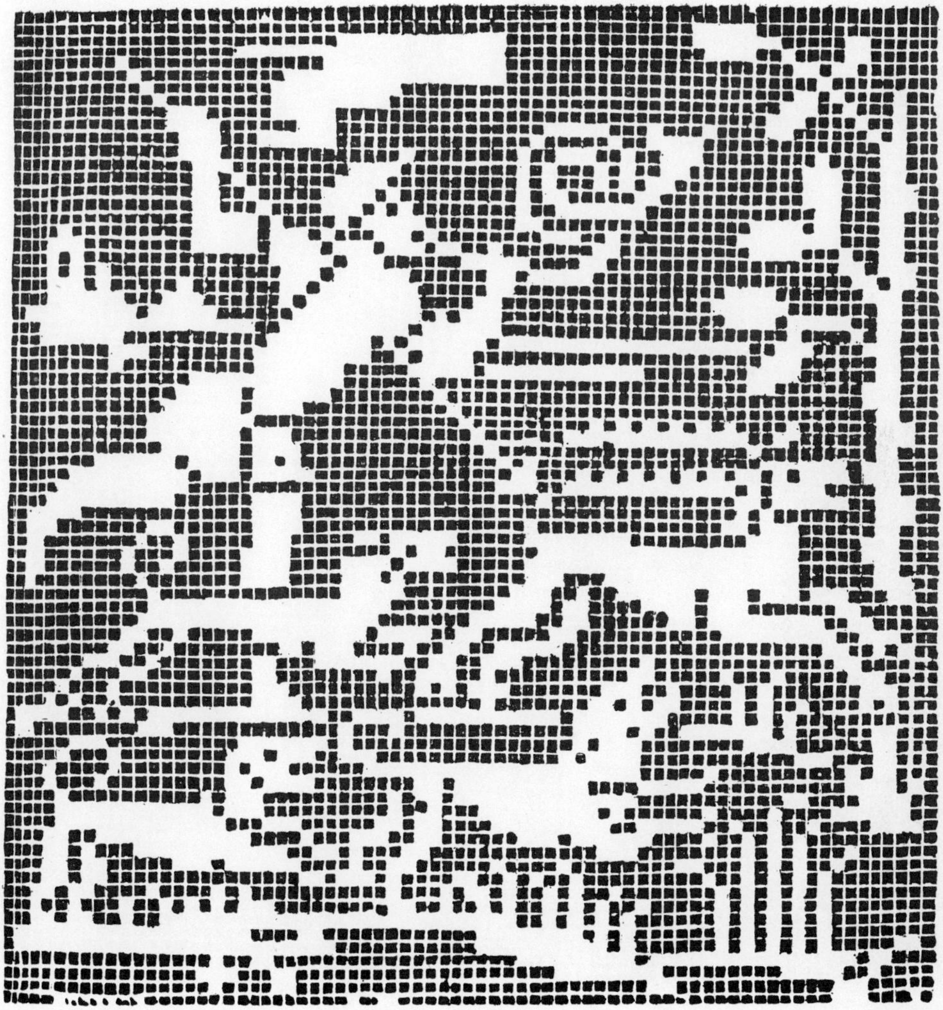

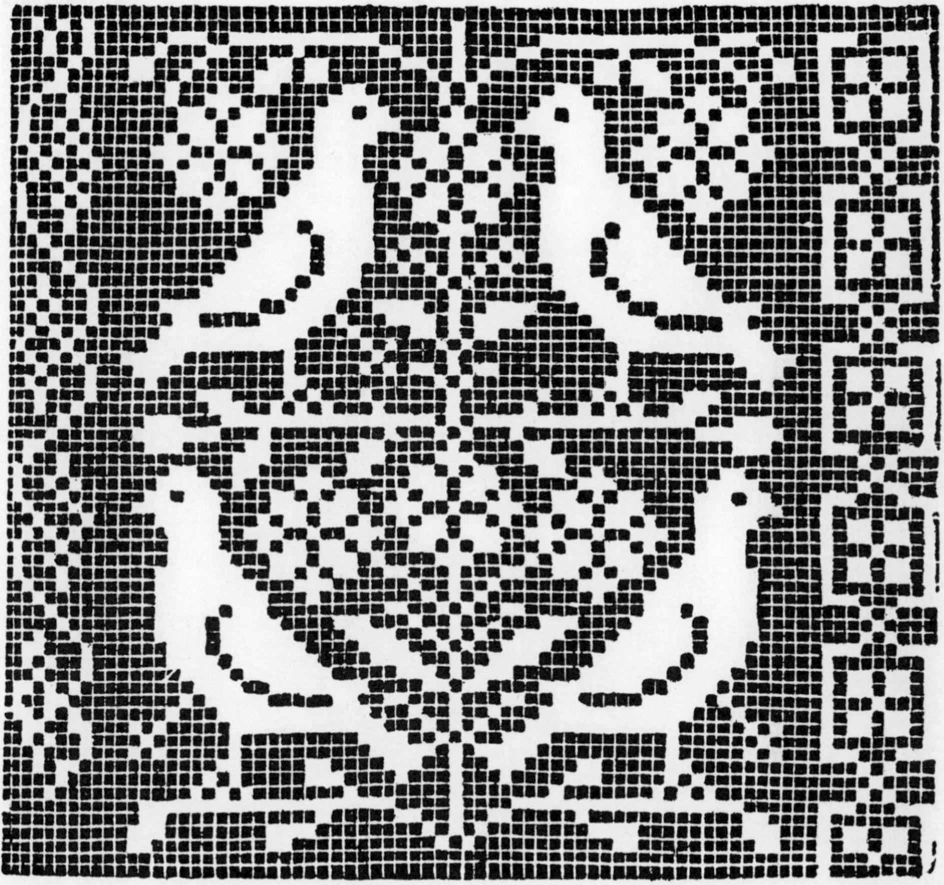

54

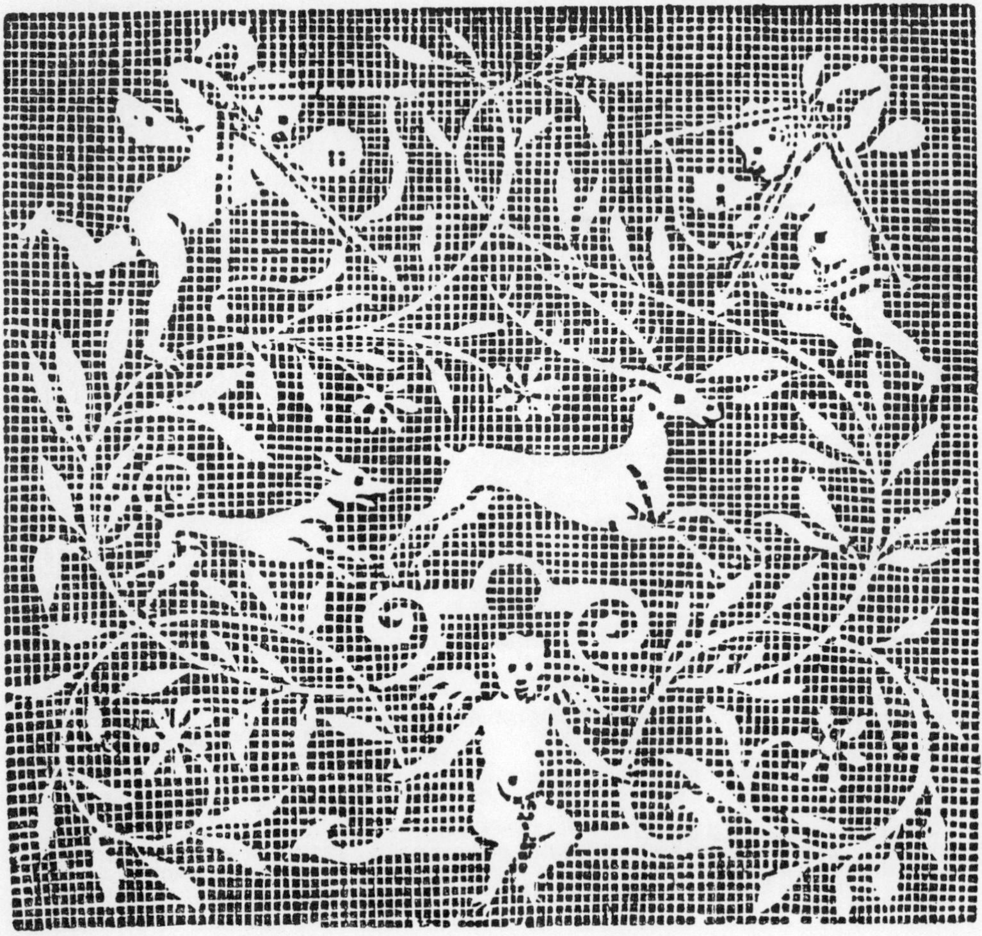

59

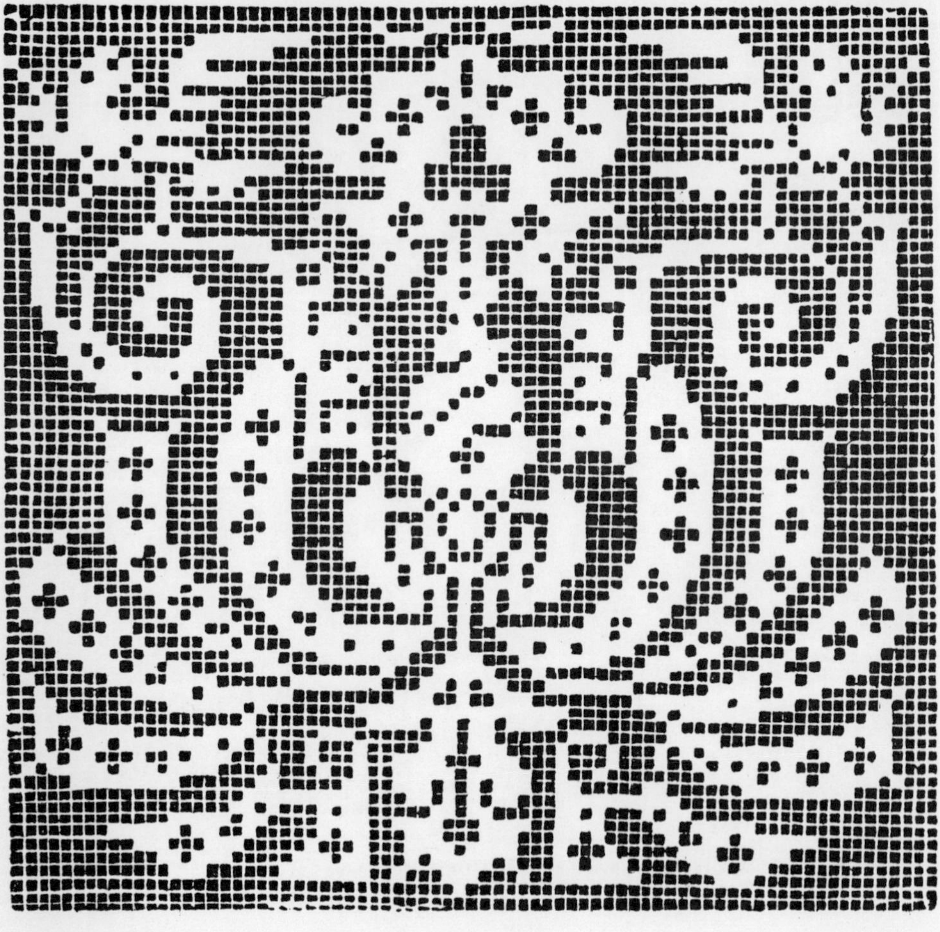

Sol.

Luna.

Mars.

Mercure.

Iuppiter.

65

Venus.

Saturne.

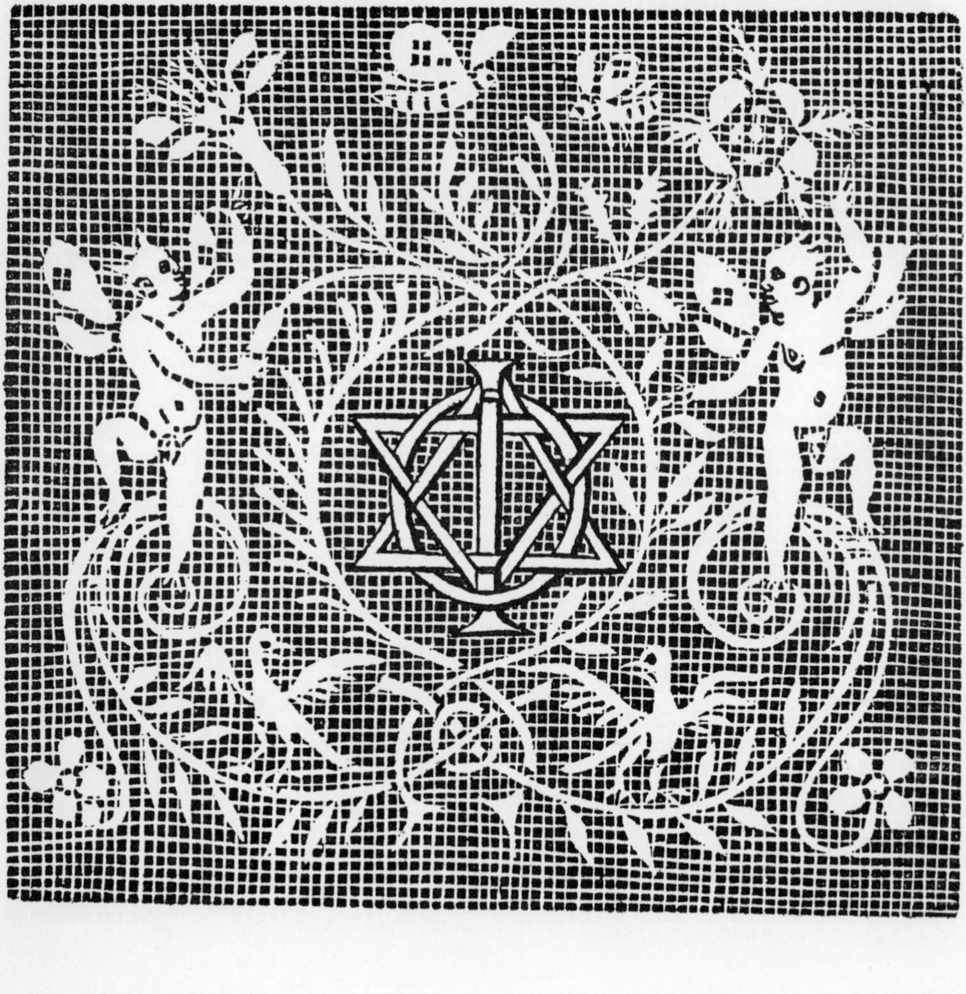

Ce quarre contient 41.maille, & la bordure 69.

This square contains 41 meshes, and the border 69.

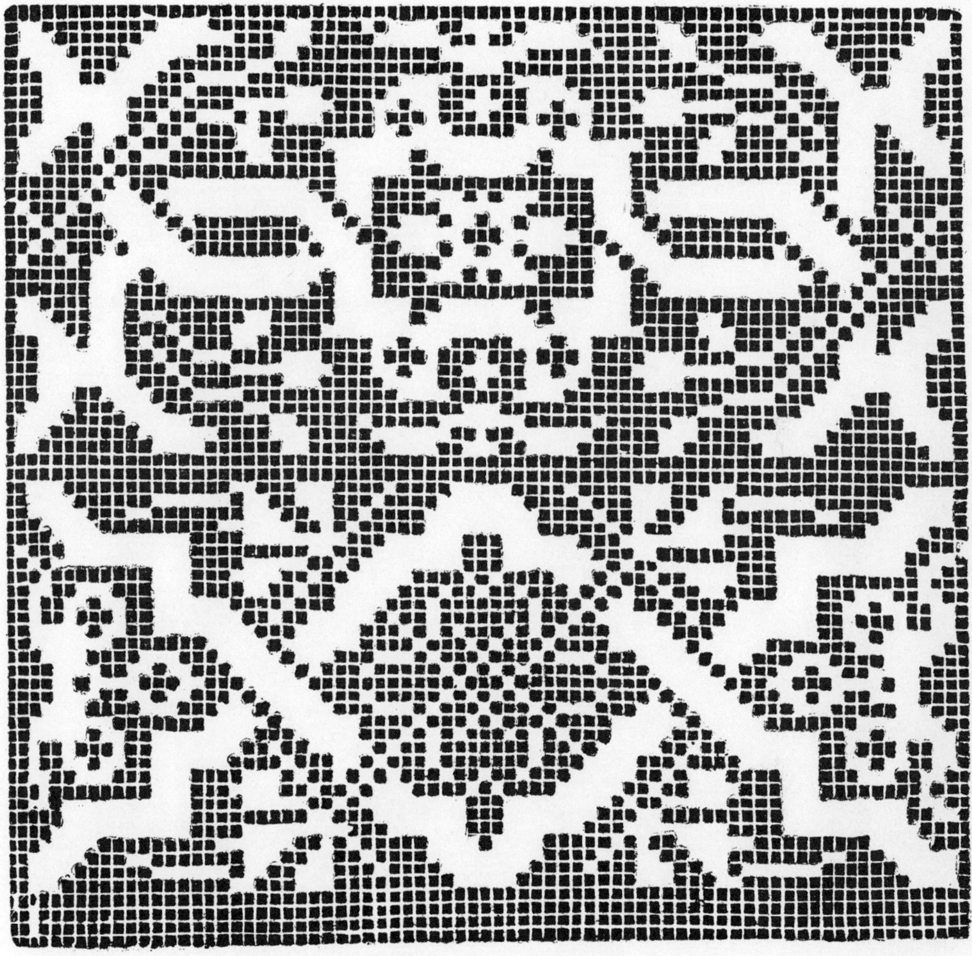

Ce quarre contient 48.mailles, & la bordure 67.

This square contains 48 meshes, and the border 67.

This square contains 63 meshes.

This square contains 41 meshes, and the border 65.

This square contains 43 meshes, and the border 67.

This square contains 65 meshes.

La Licorne côtient en hauteur 4 4.mailles, & en lógueur 6 2.

The unicorn contains 44 meshes in height, and 62 in length.

Ce coin de Mouchoir contient en largeur 35. mailles.

This handkerchief corner contains 35 meshes in width.

Ce coin de Mouchoir contient 33. mailles.

This handkerchief corner contains 33 meshes.

The border above contains 35 meshes, the one below 25.

Ce Lyon contient en hauteur 59. mailles,
& en longueur 64.

This lion contains 59 meshes in height, and 64 in length.

The border above contains 25 meshes, the one below 26.

Ce Paon contient en longueur 65.mailles, & en hauteur 61.

This peacock contains 65 meshes in length, 61 in height.

This pelican contains 70 meshes in length, 65 in height.

Ce Griffon contient en hauteur 58.mailles, & en longueur 67.

This griffin contains 58 meshes in height, 67 in length.

Ce Cerf contient en hauteur 66.mailles, & en longueur 55.

This stag contains 66 meshes in height, 55 in length.

La Deeſſe des Fleurs repreſentant le Printemps, contient en hauteur 69. mailles, & en longueur 64.

The goddess of flowers, representing Spring, contains 69 meshes
in height, 64 in length.

La Deeſſe des Bleds repreſentant l'Eſte, contient en hauteur 68. mailles , & en largeur 70.

The goddess of grain, representing Summer, contains 68 meshes
in height, 70 in length.

Ce Bachus reprefentant l'Automne, contient en hauteur, 67. mailles, & en largeur 54.

This Bacchus, representing Autumn, contains 67 meshes
in height, 54 in length.

Cefte figure reprefentant l'Hiuer, contient en
hauteur, 63. mailles, & en largeur 53.

This figure representing Winter contains 63 meshes
in height, 53 in length.

A CATALOGUE OF SELECTED DOVER BOOKS
IN ALL FIELDS OF INTEREST

A CATALOGUE OF SELECTED DOVER
BOOKS IN ALL FIELDS OF INTEREST

RACKHAM'S COLOR ILLUSTRATIONS FOR WAGNER'S RING. Rackham's finest mature work—all 64 full-color watercolors in a faithful and lush interpretation of the *Ring*. Full-sized plates on coated stock of the paintings used by opera companies for authentic staging of Wagner. Captions aid in following complete Ring cycle. Introduction. 64 illustrations plus vignettes. 72pp. 8⅝ x 11¼. 23779-6 Pa. $6.00

CONTEMPORARY POLISH POSTERS IN FULL COLOR, edited by Joseph Czestochowski. 46 full-color examples of brilliant school of Polish graphic design, selected from world's first museum (near Warsaw) dedicated to poster art. Posters on circuses, films, plays, concerts all show cosmopolitan influences, free imagination. Introduction. 48pp. 9⅜ x 12¼. 23780-X Pa. $6.00

GRAPHIC WORKS OF EDVARD MUNCH, Edvard Munch. 90 haunting, evocative prints by first major Expressionist artist and one of the greatest graphic artists of his time: *The Scream, Anxiety, Death Chamber, The Kiss, Madonna*, etc. Introduction by Alfred Werner. 90pp. 9 x 12. 23765-6 Pa. $5.00

THE GOLDEN AGE OF THE POSTER, Hayward and Blanche Cirker. 70 extraordinary posters in full colors, from Maitres de l'Affiche, Mucha, Lautrec, Bradley, Cheret, Beardsley, many others. Total of 78pp. 9⅜ x 12¼. 22753-7 Pa. $5.95

THE NOTEBOOKS OF LEONARDO DA VINCI, edited by J. P. Richter. Extracts from manuscripts reveal great genius; on painting, sculpture, anatomy, sciences, geography, etc. Both Italian and English. 186 ms. pages reproduced, plus 500 additional drawings, including studies for *Last Supper*, Sforza monument, etc. 860pp. 7⅞ x 10¾. (Available in U.S. only) 22572-0, 22573-9 Pa., Two-vol. set $15.90

THE CODEX NUTTALL, as first edited by Zelia Nuttall. Only inexpensive edition, in full color, of a pre-Columbian Mexican (Mixtec) book. 88 color plates show kings, gods, heroes, temples, sacrifices. New explanatory, historical introduction by Arthur G. Miller. 96pp. 11⅜ x 8½. (Available in U.S. only) 23168-2 Pa. $7.50

UNE SEMAINE DE BONTÉ, A SURREALISTIC NOVEL IN COLLAGE, Max Ernst. Masterpiece created out of 19th-century periodical illustrations, explores worlds of terror and surprise. Some consider this Ernst's greatest work. 208pp. 8⅛ x 11. 23252-2 Pa. $5.00

HOLLYWOOD GLAMOUR PORTRAITS, edited by John Kobal. 145 photos capture the stars from 1926-49, the high point in portrait photography. Gable, Harlow, Bogart, Bacall, Hedy Lamarr, Marlene Dietrich, Robert Montgomery, Marlon Brando, Veronica Lake; 94 stars in all. Full background on photographers, technical aspects, much more. Total of 160pp. 8⅜ x 11¼. 23352-9 Pa. $5.00

THE NEW YORK STAGE: FAMOUS PRODUCTIONS IN PHOTOGRAPHS, edited by Stanley Appelbaum. 148 photographs from Museum of City of New York show 142 plays, 1883-1939. *Peter Pan, The Front Page, Dead End, Our Town*, O'Neill, hundreds of actors and actresses, etc. Full indexes. 154pp. 9½ x 10. 23241-7 Pa. $4.50

MASTERS OF THE DRAMA, John Gassner. Most comprehensive history of the drama, every tradition from Greeks to modern Europe and America, including Orient. Covers 800 dramatists, 2000 plays; biography, plot summaries, criticism, theatre history, etc. 77 illustrations. 890pp. 5⅜ x 8½. 20100-7 Clothbd. $10.00

THE GREAT OPERA STARS IN HISTORIC PHOTOGRAPHS, edited by James Camner. 343 portraits from the 1850s to the 1940s: Tamburini, Mario, Caliapin, Jeritza, Melchior, Melba, Patti, Pinza, Schipa, Caruso, Farrar, Steber, Gobbi, and many more—270 performers in all. Index. 199pp. 8⅜ x 11¼. 23575-0 Pa. $6.50

J. S. BACH, Albert Schweitzer. Great full-length study of Bach, life, background to music, music, by foremost modern scholar. Ernest Newman translation. 650 musical examples. Total of 928pp. 5⅜ x 8½. (Available in U.S. only) 21631-4, 21632-2 Pa., Two-vol. set $9.00

COMPLETE PIANO SONATAS, Ludwig van Beethoven. All sonatas in the fine Schenker edition, with fingering, analytical material. One of best modern editions. Total of 615pp. 9 x 12. (Available in U.S. only) 23134-8, 23135-6 Pa., Two-vol. set $13.00

KEYBOARD MUSIC, J. S. Bach. Bach-Gesellschaft edition. For harpsichord, piano, other keyboard instruments. English Suites, French Suites, Six Partitas, Goldberg Variations, Two-Part Inventions, Three-Part Sinfonias. 312pp. 8⅛ x 11. (Available in U.S. only) 22360-4 Pa. $5.50

FOUR SYMPHONIES IN FULL SCORE, Franz Schubert. Schubert's four most popular symphonies: No. 4 in C Minor ("Tragic"); No. 5 in B-flat Major; No. 8 in B Minor ("Unfinished"); No. 9 in C Major ("Great"). Breitkopf & Hartel edition. Study score. 261pp. 9⅜ x 12¼. 23681-1 Pa. $6.50

THE AUTHENTIC GILBERT & SULLIVAN SONGBOOK, W. S. Gilbert, A. S. Sullivan. Largest selection available; 92 songs, uncut, original keys, in piano rendering approved by Sullivan. Favorites and lesser-known fine numbers. Edited with plot synopses by James Spero. 3 illustrations. 399pp. 9 x 12. 23482-7 Pa. $7.95

THE DEPRESSION YEARS AS PHOTOGRAPHED BY ARTHUR ROTH-STEIN, Arthur Rothstein. First collection devoted entirely to the work of outstanding 1930s photographer: famous dust storm photo, ragged children, unemployed, etc. 120 photographs. Captions. 119pp. 9¼ x 10¾.
23590-4 Pa. $5.00

CAMERA WORK: A PICTORIAL GUIDE, Alfred Stieglitz. All 559 illustrations and plates from the most important periodical in the history of art photography, *Camera Work* (1903-17). Presented four to a page, reduced in size but still clear, in strict chronological order, with complete captions. Three indexes. Glossary. Bibliography. 176pp. 8⅜ x 11¼.
23591-2 Pa. $6.95

ALVIN LANGDON COBURN, PHOTOGRAPHER, Alvin L. Coburn. Revealing autobiography by one of greatest photographers of 20th century gives insider's version of Photo-Secession, plus comments on his own work. 77 photographs by Coburn. Edited by Helmut and Alison Gernsheim. 160pp. 8⅛ x 11.
23685-4 Pa. $6.00

NEW YORK IN THE FORTIES, Andreas Feininger. 162 brilliant photographs by the well-known photographer, formerly with *Life* magazine, show commuters, shoppers, Times Square at night, Harlem nightclub, Lower East Side, etc. Introduction and full captions by John von Hartz. 181pp. 9¼ x 10¾.
23585-8 Pa. $6.00

GREAT NEWS PHOTOS AND THE STORIES BEHIND THEM, John Faber. Dramatic volume of 140 great news photos, 1855 through 1976, and revealing stories behind them, with both historical and technical information. Hindenburg disaster, shooting of Oswald, nomination of Jimmy Carter, etc. 160pp. 8¼ x 11.
23667-6 Pa. $5.00

THE ART OF THE CINEMATOGRAPHER, Leonard Maltin. Survey of American cinematography history and anecdotal interviews with 5 masters—Arthur Miller, Hal Mohr, Hal Rosson, Lucien Ballard, and Conrad Hall. Very large selection of behind-the-scenes production photos. 105 photographs. Filmographies. Index. Originally *Behind the Camera*. 144pp. 8¼ x 11.
23686-2 Pa. $5.00

DESIGNS FOR THE THREE-CORNERED HAT (LE TRICORNE), Pablo Picasso. 32 fabulously rare drawings—including 31 color illustrations of costumes and accessories—for 1919 production of famous ballet. Edited by Parmenia Migel, who has written new introduction. 48pp. 9⅜ x 12¼. (Available in U.S. only)
23709-5 Pa. $5.00

NOTES OF A FILM DIRECTOR, Sergei Eisenstein. Greatest Russian filmmaker explains montage, making of *Alexander Nevsky*, aesthetics; comments on self, associates, great rivals (Chaplin), similar material. 78 illustrations. 240pp. 5⅜ x 8½.
22392-2 Pa. $4.50

THE ANATOMY OF THE HORSE, George Stubbs. Often considered the great masterpiece of animal anatomy. Full reproduction of 1766 edition, plus prospectus; original text and modernized text. 36 plates. Introduction by Eleanor Garvey. 121pp. 11 x 14¾.   23402-9 Pa. $6.00

BRIDGMAN'S LIFE DRAWING, George B. Bridgman. More than 500 illustrative drawings and text teach you to abstract the body into its major masses, use light and shade, proportion; as well as specific areas of anatomy, of which Bridgman is master. 192pp. 6½ x 9¼. (Available in U.S. only)
22710-3 Pa. $2.50

ART NOUVEAU DESIGNS IN COLOR, Alphonse Mucha, Maurice Verneuil, Georges Auriol. Full-color reproduction of *Combinaisons ornementales* (c. 1900) by Art Nouveau masters. Floral, animal, geometric, interlacings, swashes—borders, frames, spots—all incredibly beautiful. 60 plates, hundreds of designs. 9⅜ x 8-1/16.   22885-1 Pa. $4.00

FULL-COLOR FLORAL DESIGNS IN THE ART NOUVEAU STYLE, E. A. Seguy. 166 motifs, on 40 plates, from *Les fleurs et leurs applications decoratives* (1902): borders, circular designs, repeats, allovers, "spots." All in authentic Art Nouveau colors. 48pp. 9⅜ x 12¼.
23439-8 Pa. $5.00

A DIDEROT PICTORIAL ENCYCLOPEDIA OF TRADES AND IN-DUSTRY, edited by Charles C. Gillispie. 485 most interesting plates from the great French Encyclopedia of the 18th century show hundreds of working figures, artifacts, process, land and cityscapes; glassmaking, paper-making, metal extraction, construction, weaving, making furniture, clothing, wigs, dozens of other activities. Plates fully explained. 920pp. 9 x 12.
22284-5, 22285-3 Clothbd., Two-vol. set $40.00

HANDBOOK OF EARLY ADVERTISING ART, Clarence P. Hornung. Largest collection of copyright-free early and antique advertising art ever compiled. Over 6,000 illustrations, from Franklin's time to the 1890's for special effects, novelty. Valuable source, almost inexhaustible.
Pictorial Volume. Agriculture, the zodiac, animals, autos, birds, Christmas, fire engines, flowers, trees, musical instruments, ships, games and sports, much more. Arranged by subject matter and use. 237 plates. 288pp. 9 x 12.
20122-8 Clothbd. $13.50

Typographical Volume. Roman and Gothic faces ranging from 10 point to 300 point, "Barnum," German and Old English faces, script, logotypes, scrolls and flourishes, 1115 ornamental initials, 67 complete alphabets, more. 310 plates. 320pp. 9 x 12.   20123-6 Clothbd. $13.50

CALLIGRAPHY (CALLIGRAPHIA LATINA), J. G. Schwandner. High point of 18th-century ornamental calligraphy. Very ornate initials, scrolls, borders, cherubs, birds, lettered examples. 172pp. 9 x 13.
20475-8 Pa. $6.00

DRAWINGS OF WILLIAM BLAKE, William Blake. 92 plates from Book of Job, *Divine Comedy, Paradise Lost,* visionary heads, mythological figures, Laocoon, etc. Selection, introduction, commentary by Sir Geoffrey Keynes. 178pp. 8⅛ x 11. 22303-5 Pa. $4.00

ENGRAVINGS OF HOGARTH, William Hogarth. 101 of Hogarth's greatest works: *Rake's Progress, Harlot's Progress, Illustrations for Hudibras, Before and After, Beer Street and Gin Lane,* many more. Full commentary. 256pp. 11 x 13¾. 22479-1 Pa. $7.95

DAUMIER: 120 GREAT LITHOGRAPHS, Honore Daumier. Wide-ranging collection of lithographs by the greatest caricaturist of the 19th century. Concentrates on eternally popular series on lawyers, on married life, on liberated women, etc. Selection, introduction, and notes on plates by Charles F. Ramus. Total of 158pp. 9⅜ x 12¼. 23512-2 Pa. $5.50

DRAWINGS OF MUCHA, Alphonse Maria Mucha. Work reveals draftsman of highest caliber: studies for famous posters and paintings, renderings for book illustrations and ads, etc. 70 works, 9 in color; including 6 items not drawings. Introduction. List of illustrations. 72pp. 9⅜ x 12¼. (Available in U.S. only) 23672-2 Pa. $4.00

GIOVANNI BATTISTA PIRANESI: DRAWINGS IN THE PIERPONT MORGAN LIBRARY, Giovanni Battista Piranesi. For first time ever all of Morgan Library's collection, world's largest. 167 illustrations of rare Piranesi drawings—archeological, architectural, decorative and visionary. Essay, detailed list of drawings, chronology, captions. Edited by Felice Stampfle. 144pp. 9⅜ x 12¼. 23714-1 Pa. $7.50

NEW YORK ETCHINGS (1905-1949), John Sloan. All of important American artist's N.Y. life etchings. 67 works include some of his best art; also lively historical record—Greenwich Village, tenement scenes. Edited by Sloan's widow. Introduction and captions. 79pp. 8⅜ x 11¼. 23651-X Pa. $4.00

CHINESE PAINTING AND CALLIGRAPHY: A PICTORIAL SURVEY, Wan-go Weng. 69 fine examples from John M. Crawford's matchless private collection: landscapes, birds, flowers, human figures, etc., plus calligraphy. Every basic form included: hanging scrolls, handscrolls, album leaves, fans, etc. 109 illustrations. Introduction. Captions. 192pp. 8⅞ x 11¾. 23707-9 Pa. $7.95

DRAWINGS OF REMBRANDT, edited by Seymour Slive. Updated Lippmann, Hofstede de Groot edition, with definitive scholarly apparatus. All portraits, biblical sketches, landscapes, nudes, Oriental figures, classical studies, together with selection of work by followers. 550 illustrations. Total of 630pp. 9⅛ x 12¼. 21485-0, 21486-9 Pa., Two-vol. set $14.00

THE DISASTERS OF WAR, Francisco Goya. 83 etchings record horrors of Napoleonic wars in Spain and war in general. Reprint of 1st edition, plus 3 additional plates. Introduction by Philip Hofer. 97pp. 9⅜ x 8¼. 21872-4 Pa. $3.75

THE COMPLETE BOOK OF DOLL MAKING AND COLLECTING, Catherine Christopher. Instructions, patterns for dozens of dolls, from rag doll on up to elaborate, historically accurate figures. Mould faces, sew clothing, make doll houses, etc. Also collecting information. Many illustrations. 288pp. 6 x 9. 22066-4 Pa. $4.00

THE DAGUERREOTYPE IN AMERICA, Beaumont Newhall. Wonderful portraits, 1850's townscapes, landscapes; full text plus 104 photographs. The basic book. Enlarged 1976 edition. 272pp. 8¼ x 11¼. 23322-7 Pa. $6.00

CRAFTSMAN HOMES, Gustav Stickley. 296 architectural drawings, floor plans, and photographs illustrate 40 different kinds of "Mission-style" homes from *The Craftsman* (1901-16), voice of American style of simplicity and organic harmony. Thorough coverage of Craftsman idea in text and picture, now collector's item. 224pp. 8⅛ x 11. 23791-5 Pa. $6.00

PEWTER-WORKING: INSTRUCTIONS AND PROJECTS, Burl N. Osborn. & Gordon O. Wilber. Introduction to pewter-working for amateur craftsman. History and characteristics of pewter; tools, materials, step-by-step instructions. Photos, line drawings, diagrams. Total of 160pp. 7⅞ x 10¾. 23786-9 Pa. $3.50

THE GREAT CHICAGO FIRE, edited by David Lowe. 10 dramatic, eye-witness accounts of the 1871 disaster, including one of the aftermath and rebuilding, plus 70 contemporary photographs and illustrations of the ruins—courthouse, Palmer House, Great Central Depot, etc. Introduction by David Lowe. 87pp. 8¼ x 11. 23771-0 Pa. $4.00

SILHOUETTES: A PICTORIAL ARCHIVE OF VARIED ILLUSTRATIONS, edited by Carol Belanger Grafton. Over 600 silhouettes from the 18th to 20th centuries include profiles and full figures of men and women, children, birds and animals, groups and scenes, nature, ships, an alphabet. Dozens of uses for commercial artists and craftspeople. 144pp. 8⅜ x 11¼. 23781-8 Pa. $4.00

ANIMALS: 1,419 COPYRIGHT-FREE ILLUSTRATIONS OF MAMMALS, BIRDS, FISH, INSECTS, ETC., edited by Jim Harter. Clear wood engravings present, in extremely lifelike poses, over 1,000 species of animals. One of the most extensive copyright-free pictorial sourcebooks of its kind. Captions. Index. 284pp. 9 x 12. 23766-4 Pa. $7.50

INDIAN DESIGNS FROM ANCIENT ECUADOR, Frederick W. Shaffer. 282 original designs by pre-Columbian Indians of Ecuador (500-1500 A.D.). Designs include people, mammals, birds, reptiles, fish, plants, heads, geometric designs. Use as is or alter for advertising, textiles, leathercraft, etc. Introduction. 95pp. 8¾ x 11¼. 23764-8 Pa. $3.50

SZIGETI ON THE VIOLIN, Joseph Szigeti. Genial, loosely structured tour by premier violinist, featuring a pleasant mixture of reminiscenes, insights into great music and musicians, innumerable tips for practicing violinists. 385 musical passages. 256pp. 5⅝ x 8¼. 23763-X Pa. $3.50

THE COMPLETE WOODCUTS OF ALBRECHT DURER, edited by Dr. W. Kurth. 346 in all: "Old Testament," "St. Jerome," "Passion," "Life of Virgin," Apocalypse," many others. Introduction by Campbell Dodgson. 285pp. 8½ x 12¼. 21097-9 Pa. $6.95

DRAWINGS OF ALBRECHT DURER, edited by Heinrich Wölfflin. 81 plates show development from youth to full style. Many favorites; many new. Introduction by Alfred Werner. 96pp. 8⅛ x 11. 22352-3 Pa. $4.00

THE HUMAN FIGURE, Albrecht Dürer. Experiments in various techniques—stereometric, progressive proportional, and others. Also life studies that rank among finest ever done. Complete reprinting of *Dresden Sketchbook*. 170 plates. 355pp. 8⅜ x 11¼. 21042-1 Pa. $6.95

OF THE JUST SHAPING OF LETTERS, Albrecht Dürer. Renaissance artist explains design of Roman majuscules by geometry, also Gothic lower and capitals. Grolier Club edition. 43pp. 7⅞ x 10¾ 21306-4 Pa. $2.50

TEN BOOKS ON ARCHITECTURE, Vitruvius. The most important book ever written on architecture. Early Roman aesthetics, technology, classical orders, site selection, all other aspects. Stands behind everything since. Morgan translation. 331pp. 5⅜ x 8½. 20645-9 Pa. $3.75

THE FOUR BOOKS OF ARCHITECTURE, Andrea Palladio. 16th-century classic responsible for Palladian movement and style. Covers classical architectural remains, Renaissance revivals, classical orders, etc. 1738 Ware English edition. Introduction by A. Placzek. 216 plates. 110pp. of text. 9½ x 12¾. 21308-0 Pa. $7.50

HORIZONS, Norman Bel Geddes. Great industrialist stage designer, "father of streamlining," on application of aesthetics to transportation, amusement, architecture, etc. 1932 prophetic account; function, theory, specific projects. 222 illustrations. 312pp. 7⅞ x 10¾. 23514-9 Pa. $6.95

FRANK LLOYD WRIGHT'S FALLINGWATER, Donald Hoffmann. Full, illustrated story of conception and building of Wright's masterwork at Bear Run, Pa. 100 photographs of site, construction, and details of completed structure. 112pp. 9¼ x 10. 23671-4 Pa. $5.00

THE ELEMENTS OF DRAWING, John Ruskin. Timeless classic by great Viltorian; starts with basic ideas, works through more difficult. Many practical exercises. 48 illustrations. Introduction by Lawrence Campbell. 228pp. 5⅜ x 8½. 22730-8 Pa. $2.75

GIST OF ART, John Sloan. Greatest modern American teacher, Art Students League, offers innumerable hints, instructions, guided comments to help you in painting. Not a formal course. 46 illustrations. Introduction by Helen Sloan. 200pp. 5⅜ x 8½. 23435-5 Pa. $3.50

THE EARLY WORK OF AUBREY BEARDSLEY, Aubrey Beardsley. 157 plates, 2 in color: *Manon Lescaut, Madame Bovary, Morte Darthur, Salome,* other. Introduction by H. Marillier. 182pp. 8⅛ x 11. 21816-3 Pa. $4.50

THE LATER WORK OF AUBREY BEARDSLEY, Aubrey Beardsley. Exotic masterpieces of full maturity: *Venus and Tannhauser, Lysistrata, Rape of the Lock, Volpone,* Savoy material, etc. 174 plates, 2 in color. 186pp. 8⅛ x 11. 21817-1 Pa. $4.50

THOMAS NAST'S CHRISTMAS DRAWINGS, Thomas Nast. Almost all Christmas drawings by creator of image of Santa Claus as we know it, and one of America's foremost illustrators and political cartoonists. 66 illustrations. 3 illustrations in color on covers. 96pp. 8⅜ x 11¼. 23660-9 Pa. $3.50

THE DORÉ ILLUSTRATIONS FOR DANTE'S DIVINE COMEDY, Gustave Doré. All 135 plates from Inferno, Purgatory, Paradise; fantastic tortures, infernal landscapes, celestial wonders. Each plate with appropriate (translated) verses. 141pp. 9 x 12. 23231-X Pa. $4.50

DORÉ'S ILLUSTRATIONS FOR RABELAIS, Gustave Doré. 252 striking illustrations of *Gargantua and Pantagruel* books by foremost 19th-century illustrator. Including 60 plates, 192 delightful smaller illustrations. 153pp. 9 x 12. 23656-0 Pa. $5.00

LONDON: A PILGRIMAGE, Gustave Doré, Blanchard Jerrold. Squalor, riches, misery, beauty of mid-Victorian metropolis; 55 wonderful plates, 125 other illustrations, full social, cultural text by Jerrold. 191pp. of text. 9⅜ x 12¼. 22306-X Pa. $6.00

THE RIME OF THE ANCIENT MARINER, Gustave Doré, S. T. Coleridge. Dore's finest work, 34 plates capture moods, subtleties of poem. Full text. Introduction by Millicent Rose. 77pp. 9¼ x 12. 22305-1 Pa. $3.00

THE DORE BIBLE ILLUSTRATIONS, Gustave Doré. All wonderful, detailed plates: Adam and Eve, Flood, Babylon, Life of Jesus, etc. Brief King James text with each plate. Introduction by Millicent Rose. 241 plates. 241pp. 9 x 12. 23004-X Pa. $5.00

THE COMPLETE ENGRAVINGS, ETCHINGS AND DRYPOINTS OF ALBRECHT DURER. "Knight, Death and Devil"; "Melencolia," and more—all Dürer's known works in all three media, including 6 works formerly attributed to him. 120 plates. 235pp. 8⅜ x 11¼. 22851-7 Pa. $6.50

MAXIMILIAN'S TRIUMPHAL ARCH, Albrecht Dürer and others. Incredible monument of woodcut art: 8 foot high elaborate arch—heraldic figures, humans, battle scenes, fantastic elements—that you can assemble yourself. Printed on one side, layout for assembly. 143pp. 11 x 16. 21451-6 Pa. $5.00

"OSCAR" OF THE WALDORF'S COOKBOOK, Oscar Tschirky. Famous American chef reveals 3455 recipes that made Waldorf great; cream of French, German, American cooking, in all categories. Full instructions, easy home use. 1896 edition. 907pp. 6⅝ x 9⅜.   20790-0 Clothbd. $15.00

COOKING WITH BEER, Carole Fahy. Beer has as superb an effect on food as wine, and at fraction of cost. Over 250 recipes for appetizers, soups, main dishes, desserts, breads, etc. Index. 144pp. 5⅜ x 8½. (Available in U.S. only)   23661-7 Pa. $2.50

STEWS AND RAGOUTS, Kay Shaw Nelson. This international cookbook offers wide range of 108 recipes perfect for everyday, special occasions, meals-in-themselves, main dishes. Economical, nutritious, easy-to-prepare: goulash, Irish stew, boeuf bourguignon, etc. Index. 134pp. 5⅜ x 8½.
                                                           23662-5 Pa. $2.50

DELICIOUS MAIN COURSE DISHES, Marian Tracy. Main courses are the most important part of any meal. These 200 nutritious, economical recipes from around the world make every meal a delight. "I . . . have found it so useful in my own household,"—*N.Y. Times.* Index. 219pp. 5⅜ x 8½.   23664-1 Pa. $3.00

FIVE ACRES AND INDEPENDENCE, Maurice G. Kains. Great back-to-the-land classic explains basics of self-sufficient farming: economics, plants, crops, animals, orchards, soils, land selection, host of other necessary things. Do not confuse with skimpy faddist literature; Kains was one of America's greatest agriculturalists. 95 illustrations. 397pp. 5⅜ x 8½.
                                                           20974-1 Pa. $3.50

A PRACTICAL GUIDE FOR THE BEGINNING FARMER, Herbert Jacobs. Basic, extremely useful first book for anyone thinking about moving to the country and starting a farm. Simpler than Kains, with greater emphasis on country living in general. 246pp. 5⅜ x 8½.
                                                           23675-7 Pa. $3.50

HARDY BULBS, Louise Beebe Wilder. Fullest, most thorough book on plants grown from bulbs, corms, rhizomes and tubers. 40 genera and 335 species covered: selecting, cultivating, naturalizing; name, origins, blooming season, when to plant, special requirements. 127 illustrations. 432pp. 5⅜ x 8½.   23102-X Pa. $4.50

A GARDEN OF PLEASANT FLOWERS (PARADISI IN SOLE: PARADISUS TERRESTRIS), John Parkinson. Complete, unabridged reprint of first (1629) edition of earliest great English book on gardens and gardening. More than 1000 plants & flowers of Elizabethan, Jacobean garden fully described, most with woodcut illustrations. Botanically very reliable, a "speaking garden" of exceeding charm. 812 illustrations. 628pp. 8½ x 12¼.   23392-8 Clothbd. $25.00

THE AMERICAN SENATOR, Anthony Trollope. Little known, long un-available Trollope novel on a grand scale. Here are humorous comment on American vs. English culture, and stunning portrayal of a heroine/villainess. Superb evocation of Victorian village life. 561pp. 5⅜ x 8½.
23801-6 Pa. $6.00

WAS IT MURDER? James Hilton. The author of *Lost Horizon* and *Good-bye, Mr. Chips* wrote one detective novel (under a pen-name) which was quickly forgotten and virtually lost, even at the height of Hilton's fame. This edition brings it back—a finely crafted public school puzzle resplen-dent with Hilton's stylish atmosphere. A thoroughly English thriller by the creator of Shangri-la. 252pp. 5⅜ x 8. (Available in U.S. only)
23774-5 Pa. $3.00

CENTRAL PARK: A PHOTOGRAPHIC GUIDE, Victor Laredo and Henry Hope Reed. 121 superb photographs show dramatic views of Central Park: Bethesda Fountain, Cleopatra's Needle, Sheep Meadow, the Blockhouse, plus people engaged in many park activities: ice skating, bike riding, etc. Captions by former Curator of Central Park, Henry Hope Reed, provide historical view, changes, etc. Also photos of N.Y. landmarks on park's periphery. 96pp. 8½ x 11. 23750-8 Pa. $4.50

NANTUCKET IN THE NINETEENTH CENTURY, Clay Lancaster. 180 rare photographs, stereographs, maps, drawings and floor plans recreate unique American island society. Authentic scenes of shipwreck, light-houses, streets, homes are arranged in geographic sequence to provide walking-tour guide to old Nantucket existing today. Introduction, captions. 160pp. 8⅞ x 11¾. 23747-8 Pa. $6.95

STONE AND MAN: A PHOTOGRAPHIC EXPLORATION, Andreas Feininger. 106 photographs by *Life* photographer Feininger portray man's deep passion for stone through the ages. Stonehenge-like megaliths, forti-fied towns, sculpted marble and crumbling tenements show textures, beau-ties, fascination. 128pp. 9¼ x 10¾. 23756-7 Pa. $5.95

CIRCLES, A MATHEMATICAL VIEW, D. Pedoe. Fundamental aspects of college geometry, non-Euclidean geometry, and other branches of mathe-matics: representing circle by point. Poincare model, isoperimetric prop-erty, etc. Stimulating recreational reading. 66 figures. 96pp. 5⅝ x 8¼.
63698-4 Pa. $2.75

THE DISCOVERY OF NEPTUNE, Morton Grosser. Dramatic scientific history of the investigations leading up to the actual discovery of the eighth planet of our solar system. Lucid, well-researched book by well-known historian of science. 172pp. 5⅜ x 8½. 23726-5 Pa. $3.00

THE DEVIL'S DICTIONARY. Ambrose Bierce. Barbed, bitter, brilliant witticisms in the form of a dictionary. Best, most ferocious satire America has produced. 145pp. 5⅜ x 8½. 20487-1 Pa. $1.75

CATALOGUE OF DOVER BOOKS

THE SENSE OF BEAUTY, George Santayana. Masterfully written discussion of nature of beauty, materials of beauty, form, expression; art, literature, social sciences all involved. 168pp. 5⅜ x 8½. 20238-0 Pa. $2.50

ON THE IMPROVEMENT OF THE UNDERSTANDING, Benedict Spinoza. Also contains *Ethics, Correspondence,* all in excellent R. Elwes translation. Basic works on entry to philosophy, pantheism, exchange of ideas with great contemporaries. 402pp. 5⅜ x 8½. 20250-X Pa. $3.75

THE TRAGIC SENSE OF LIFE, Miguel de Unamuno. Acknowledged masterpiece of existential literature, one of most important books of 20th century. Introduction by Madariaga. 367pp. 5⅜ x 8½.
20257-7 Pa. $3.50

THE GUIDE FOR THE PERPLEXED, Moses Maimonides. Great classic of medieval Judaism attempts to reconcile revealed religion (Pentateuch, commentaries) with Aristotelian philosophy. Important historically, still relevant in problems. Unabridged Friedlander translation. Total of 473pp. 5⅜ x 8½. 20351-4 Pa. $5.00

THE I CHING (THE BOOK OF CHANGES), translated by James Legge. Complete translation of basic text plus appendices by Confucius, and Chinese commentary of most penetrating divination manual ever prepared. Indispensable to study of early Oriental civilizations, to modern inquiring reader. 448pp. 5⅜ x 8½. 21062-6 Pa. $4.00

THE EGYPTIAN BOOK OF THE DEAD, E. A. Wallis Budge. Complete reproduction of Ani's papyrus, finest ever found. Full hieroglyphic text, interlinear transliteration, word for word translation, smooth translation. Basic work, for Egyptology, for modern study of psychic matters. Total of 533pp. 6½ x 9¼. (Available in U.S. only) 21866-X Pa. $4.95

THE GODS OF THE EGYPTIANS, E. A. Wallis Budge. Never excelled for richness, fullness: all gods, goddesses, demons, mythical figures of Ancient Egypt; their legends, rites, incarnations, variations, powers, etc. Many hieroglyphic texts cited. Over 225 illustrations, plus 6 color plates. Total of 988pp. 6⅛ x 9¼. (Available in U.S. only)
22055-9, 22056-7 Pa., Two-vol. set $12.00

THE ENGLISH AND SCOTTISH POPULAR BALLADS, Francis J. Child. Monumental, still unsuperseded; all known variants of Child ballads, commentary on origins, literary references, Continental parallels, other features. Added: papers by G. L. Kittredge, W. M. Hart. Total of 2761pp. 6½ x 9¼.
21409-5, 21410-9, 21411-7, 21412-5, 21413-3 Pa., Five-vol. set $37.50

CORAL GARDENS AND THEIR MAGIC, Bronsilaw Malinowski. Classic study of the methods of tilling the soil and of agricultural rites in the Trobriand Islands of Melanesia. Author is one of the most important figures in the field of modern social anthropology. 143 illustrations. Indexes. Total of 911pp. of text. 5⅝ x 8¼. (Available in U.S. only)
23597-1 Pa. $12.95

THE STANDARD BOOK OF QUILT MAKING AND COLLECTING, Marguerite Ickis. Full information, full-sized patterns for making 46 traditional quilts, also 150 other patterns. Quilted cloths, lame, satin quilts, etc. 483 illustrations. 273pp. 6⅞ x 9⅝. 20582-7 Pa. $3.95

ENCYCLOPEDIA OF VICTORIAN NEEDLEWORK, S. Caulfield, Blanche Saward. Simply inexhaustible gigantic alphabetical coverage of every traditional needlecraft—stitches, materials, methods, tools, types of work; definitions, many projects to be made. 1200 illustrations; double-columned text. 697pp. 8⅛ x 11. 22800-2, 22801-0 Pa., Two-vol. set $12.00

MECHANICK EXERCISES ON THE WHOLE ART OF PRINTING, Joseph Moxon. First complete book (1683-4) ever written about typography, a compendium of everything known about printing at the latter part of 17th century. Reprint of 2nd (1962) Oxford Univ. Press edition. 74 illustrations. Total of 550pp. 6⅛ x 9¼. 23617-X Pa. $7.95

PAPERMAKING, Dard Hunter. Definitive book on the subject by the foremost authority in the field. Chapters dealing with every aspect of history of craft in every part of the world. Over 320 illustrations. 2nd, revised and enlarged (1947) edition. 672pp. 5⅜ x 8½. 23619-6 Pa. $7.95

THE ART DECO STYLE, edited by Theodore Menten. Furniture, jewelry, metalwork, ceramics, fabrics, lighting fixtures, interior decors, exteriors, graphics from pure French sources. Best sampling around. Over 400 photographs. 183pp. 8⅜ x 11¼. 22824-X Pa. $5.00

Prices subject to change without notice.

Available at your book dealer or write for free catalogue to Dept. GI, Dover Publications, Inc., 180 Varick St., N.Y., N.Y. 10014. Dover publishes more than 175 books each year on science, elementary and advanced mathematics, biology, music, art, literary history, social sciences and other areas.